The AI Survival Guide for Small to Mid-Sized Businesses

By Chad Markham

Copyright © 2026 by Chad Markham
All rights reserved.

No part of this publication may be reproduced, distributed, or transmitted in any form or by any means, including photocopying, recording, or other electronic or mechanical methods, without prior written permission of the publisher, except in the case of brief quotations used in reviews or other noncommercial uses permitted by copyright law.

For permission requests, please contact the author through allegiantdigital.com.

The AI Survival Guide for Small to Mid-Sized Businesses
First Edition
ISBN: 979-8-9936914-2-8
Printed in the United States of America

Disclaimer:
This book is a work of nonfiction. Every effort has been made to ensure the accuracy of the information presented at the time of publication. However, technology and digital marketing platforms change frequently. The author and publisher make no guarantees regarding specific outcomes and assume no responsibility for actions taken based on the contents of this book. Readers are encouraged to consult professional advisors before making significant business or marketing decisions.

DEDICATION

To the business owners who refuse to stand still.

To the ones who built something from nothing, who carry the weight of payroll, reputation, and responsibility every day.

This guide is for you.

ACKNOWLEDGMENTS

No business owner succeeds alone.

Thank you to the team at Allegiant Digital Marketing for constantly staying ahead of change and helping our clients adapt with confidence.

Thank you to the business owners who ask tough questions, challenge assumptions, and push for better answers. Your curiosity is what makes progress possible.

And thank you to every small and mid-sized business owner navigating today's fast-moving digital world. Your willingness to learn and adapt is what keeps your companies strong.

Special Acknowledgements

A special thank you to the team members who directly contributed to the creation of this book through endless hours of research, years of learned expertise, editing, fact-checking, creative design, and a myriad of other things that go into a work like this. In alphabetical order, I'd like to thank: Joel Brown, Chase Buys, Marisela Cabuto, Madison Castleberry, Madison Cherry, Sarah Fontaine, John Hansen, Will Holt, Frank LoGiudice, Indu Mariarajan, Jana Matkovic Dedic, Jason McLellan, Tito Romero, Karina San Roman, Skylar Scott, Chelsea Tash, Mike Small, Chris Tucker, Bhoomi Vazir, Sydney Vragel.

Why This Book Exists

My name is Chad Markham, president and CEO of Allegiant Digital Marketing. For years, our team has worked alongside business owners across a wide range of industries, including home services, professional services, retail, e-commerce, and more, helping them stay competitive in a constantly changing digital landscape.

Over the last few years, one topic has dominated every conversation: AI.

Artificial intelligence is no longer some distant future concept. It's already built into search engines, advertising platforms, analytics tools, and content systems. It's shaping how customers find businesses. It influences which ads are shown. It decides which websites get visibility.

And for many business owners, it feels overwhelming.

This book is not a technical deep dive. It is not a programming manual. It is not a hype piece promising overnight success.

It is a survival guide.

That means we focus on what matters, why it matters, and what you need to understand to make smart decisions. Nothing more. Nothing less.

My goal is not to turn you into a marketing expert or an AI engineer. My goal is to make sure you are never left in the dark.

When you understand how AI is changing search, ads, content, and customer behavior, you can ask better questions. You can spot red flags. You can choose the right partners. And most importantly, you can protect and grow your business with confidence.

Technology will keep changing. That part is guaranteed.

What doesn't have to change is your ability to stay informed and in control.

Thank you for reading.

If our team can ever support your growth, you can reach us at:

info@allegiantdigital.com
866-298-1910

— Chad Markham

Contents

INTRODUCTION 19

Chapter 1: Welcome to the Age of Intelligent Marketing 21

    A Decade of Disruption 21

    Why This Moment Feels Different 21

    From Search Bars to Conversations 22

    The Power Shift in Visibility 22

    What "Invisible" Really Means 23

    How Small Businesses Can Still Win 23

    Humans and Machines: The New Middle Ground 24

    Adapting Before You Have To 24

    Takeaway Summary 24

    AI Tools to Explore 25

        ChatGPT 25

        Perplexity AI 25

        Google Gemini 25

        Claude AI 26

        Midjourney 26

Chapter 2: Search Evolved: From Keywords to Intelligence 27

    A Brief History of Search Algorithms 27

    How AI Changed the Meaning of Relevance 27

Context Over Keywords 27
Semantic Search and Entity Recognition 28
Conversational Search Arrives 28
Voice Search as the Ultimate Long-Tail Play 29
Natural Language and the Death of Exact Match 29
Intent-Driven Optimization in Plain English 29
Zero-Click Search and What It Means for Visibility.... 30
Human Content That AI Can Interpret..................... 30
Takeaway Summary 31
AI Tools to Explore 32
    Google Search Console 32
    AlsoAsked... 32
    AnswerThePublic.. 32
    ChatGPT 32
    Semrush... 32

Chapter 3: Generative Search and the Rise of GEO 33
What Is Generative Engine Optimization? 33
From Web Pages to AI Summaries........................... 33
How Google, ChatGPT, and Perplexity Pull Their Sources 34
Content Depth vs. Surface-Level Answers 34
Training the Machine to Quote You 35
On Consistent Branding 35

Authority Signals That Feed AI Responses 36

Structured Data, Schema, and Citation Control 36

Real-World Example: How One Article Became a Top AI Answer 37

Balancing Brand Voice with Machine Readability 38

Being Unique and Accurate 38

Takeaway Summary 39

AI Tools to Explore 40

    Google Search Generative Experience 40

    Perplexity AI 40

    Schema.org 40

    Yoast SEO 40

    SurferSEO 40

Chapter 4: Answer Engines and the New SEO Frontier .. 41

Defining Answer Engine Optimization 41

From FAQ Pages to Conversational Content 42

Voice Assistants & Smart Tech as Gatekeepers 42

Writing for Natural Speech Patterns 42

"Who," "What," and "How" as Ranking Triggers 43

Long-Tail Conversations and AI Memory 43

Featured Snippets vs. AI Responses 44

Accuracy and Trust Signals in Voice Results 44

Optimizing for Micro-Moments and Local Intention .. 45

Integrating AEO into Your Existing SEO Playbook 45

Takeaway Summary 45

AI Tools to Explore 46

Chapter 5: Paid Media in the AI Age 47

How AI Rewrote the Ad Auction 47

Performance Max and Smart Bidding Explained 47

Local Services Ads and AI Trust Metrics 48

Predictive Budget Allocation 48

Creative Testing Without Manual A/B Work............... 48

AI Forecasting Conversions Before They Happen 49

Human Oversight in Automated Ad Campaigns 49

The Myth of "Set and Forget" Automation 49

Real-World Examples of ROI Shifts 50

Balancing Data and Gut Instinct 50

Takeaway Summary 51

AI Tools to Explore 51

    Google Ads Performance Max............................. 51

    Meta Advantage+ 51

    Microsoft Advertising Automation 51

    Optmyzr... 52

    AdCreative.ai 52

Chapter 6: The Creative Revolution: Design, Video, and Branding in the AI Era 53

The Role of Designers in an Automated World 53

From Stock Art to Synthetic Art 53

How Tools Like Midjourney and Runway Changed Design Speed 54

Visual Branding in the Age of Infinite Variation 54

Prompt Design as the New Creative Skill 54

Ethics and Copyright in AI Imagery 55

AI Video Generation and Storytelling 55

Human Emotion as a Design Advantage 56

Combining Data and Aesthetics for Higher Engagement 56

Curating AI Outputs for Brand Consistency 56

How to Integrate AI into Your Creative Team 57

Takeaway Summary 57

AI Tools to Explore 58

    Midjourney 58

    Runway ML 58

    Adobe Firefly 58

    Canva Magic Studio 58

    Pika Labs 58

Chapter 7: Content Creation in the Age of Machines 59

The AI Writer as Your Co-Author 59

Two Categories of AI 59

Prompt Engineering 101 for Marketers 60

Structuring Content That AI and Humans Both Love . 61

Voice Search and Conversational Copywriting 61

Maintaining Tone and Brand Authenticity 62

Editorial Oversight and Human Editing for AI Drafts .. 62

Content Layering: Depth Over Quantity 62

Repurposing AI-Generated Assets Across Formats ... 63

Detecting and Fixing AI Hallucinations 63

A Look at Common AI Trends to Watch Out For 64

Perfecting the Prompt 65

Let's combine what we know about developing the ideal prompt to get good, clear, accurate content via AI without making it obvious that AI was used. 65

When to Use AI and When to Write It Yourself........... 65

Takeaway Summary 66

AI Tools to Explore 66

    ChatGPT 66

    Jasper 66

    Grammarly 66

    Copy.ai 66

    QuillBot 66

Chapter 8: Social Media: Where AI Meets Emotion....... 67

Algorithms That Know You Better Than You Do.......... 67

How AI Predicts Viral Content 67

Social Listening and Sentiment Analysis 68

Conversational AI in Customer Engagement 68

AI-Generated Reels, Shorts, and Posts 68

The Rise of Chatbots That Sound Like People 69

Timing and Frequency: AI's Predictive Scheduling 69

Community Building With Authentic Responses 70

Ethical Boundaries in AI Influencer Marketing 70

From Metrics to Meaning: Humanizing Data............. 70

Takeaway Summary 71

AI Tools to Explore.. 71

    Hootsuite OwlyWriter AI.. 71

    Lately AI... 72

    Brandwatch 72

    Manychat 72

    Predis.ai 72

Chapter 9: Predictive Analytics and Personalization..... 73

What Predictive Analytics Really Means 73

Machine Learning & Behavioral Modeling in Action... 73

How AI Anticipates Customer Needs....................... 74

Voice Data as a Goldmine for Intent Insights............ 74

Building Profiles Without Third-Party Cookies 74

First-Party Data and Ethical Collection 75

Dynamic Personalization Across Channels 75

Automation That Still Feels Personal 76

The New Privacy Playbook: Transparency & Trust 76

Using Predictive Insights to Drive Real Decisions 76

Takeaway Summary 77

AI Tools to Explore 77

    HubSpot AI 77

    Google Analytics 4 (GA4) 77

    Segment 78

    Pega Customer Decision Hub 78

    Levity AI 78

Chapter 10: The Human Advantage: Where Machines Still Need Us 79

Why Empathy Can't Be Automated 79

Creative Instinct vs. Algorithmic Logic 79

Building Trust Through Storytelling 79

Human Touchpoints in Automated Journeys 80

Leadership in the AI Transition 80

Upskilling Your Team for Hybrid Workflows 80

The Emotional Side of Adoption and Change 81

Turning Fear of AI into Curiosity 81

Culture as a Competitive Edge 81

Re-Humanizing Marketing Before It's Too Late 82

Takeaway Summary 83

AI Tools to Explore 84

- Notion AI 84
- Miro 84
- Otter.ai 84
- Google Workspace AI Features 84
- Trello with Butler Automation 84

Chapter 11: Building Your AI-Ready Marketing Strategy 85

- Assessing Your Current AI Readiness 85
- Auditing Tools and Platforms You Already Use 85
- Creating a Cross-Channel AI Integration Plan 86
- Budgeting for Technology and Training 86
- Defining KPIs for AI-Assisted Performance 86
- Choosing the Right Partners and Vendors 87
- Building Internal Buy-In and Change Management ... 87
- Testing and Iterating Before Scaling 87
- Avoiding Common AI Adoption Pitfalls 88
- You're The Boss 88
- Sustaining Momentum via Continuous Learning 88
- Takeaway Summary 89
- AI Tools to Explore 89
  - Zapier 89
  - HubSpot AI 89
  - Airtable 89
  - Google Looker Studio 90

Asana Intelligence 90
Chapter 12: The Next Five Years: Where We're Headed. 91
   AI's Next Leap: From Assistants to Advisors 91
   Search, Chat, and Commerce Merge 91
   Voice Search Becomes the Default Interface 92
   Artificial General Intelligence (AGI) and Marketing Automation 92
   Regulation and Ethics in a Machine-Led World 92
   New Marketing Roles That Will Emerge 93
   Preparing for the Disappearance of Traditional Search 93
   Human Brands That Win in the AI Economy 94
   How to Stay Ahead When Change Never Stops 94
   Final Reflection: Visibility Is the New Currency 94
   Takeaway Summary 95
   AI Tools to Explore 95
      Perplexity AI 95
      ChatGPT 95
      Google Gemini 96
      Runway ML 96
      Ethical OS Toolkit 96
Adapt or Become Invisible 97
   The Moment We're In 97
   What Has Changed 97

    What Hasn't Changed 98

    The Human Role Moving Forward 98

    Building for the Future 99

    How to Stay Visible 99

    Reframing the Relationship with AI 100

    The New Definition of Success 100

    The Invisible Risk 100

    The Path Forward 101

    The Last Word 101

    Takeaway Summary 102

Author's Note 103

Recommended Resources 105

    AI and Digital Marketing Tools 105

        ChatGPT 105

        Perplexity AI 105

        Google Gemini 105

        Jasper 105

        HubSpot AI 105

    SEO and Generative Search 105

        Search Engine Journal 105

        Moz Blog 106

        Google Search Central 106

        BrightLocal 106

- Schema.org 106
- Advertising and PPC 106
  - Google Ads Help Center 106
  - Optmyzr 106
  - Meta Business Help 107
  - Microsoft Advertising Blog 107
- Creative and Visual AI 107
  - Midjourney 107
  - Runway ML 107
  - Adobe Firefly 107
  - Canva Magic Studio 107
- Learning and Continuing Education 108
  - Marketing AI Institute 108
  - Think with Google 108
  - Coursera AI for Everyone 108
  - Harvard Business Review 108

INTRODUCTION

Why This Guide Matters Right Now

If you own a small or mid-sized business, you've already felt it.

Search results look different. Ads behave differently. Content gets created faster than ever. Tools promise automation and instant growth. Everyone is talking about Artificial Intelligence... or, as everyone knows it today, AI.

Some of it is helpful. Some of it is noise.

Artificial intelligence is now part of nearly every digital platform your business depends on. Google uses it to rank websites and match ads. Social platforms use it to determine visibility. Email tools use it to predict behavior. Analytics systems use it to forecast trends.

Whether you actively use AI or not, it is already influencing your business.

That is why this book exists.

You do not need to master machine learning. You do not need to write code. You do not need to chase every new tool that launches.

What you do need is clarity.

In the chapters ahead, you will learn:

- How AI is changing search and online visibility
- How advertising platforms now rely on machine

learning
- How content creation has shifted
- How customer behavior is evolving
- What to watch for in the coming years
- How to stay competitive without losing your voice

This is not a do-it-yourself technical manual. It is a practical guide to help you understand what is happening so you can make smarter decisions.

If you run a local service company, a retail brand, an online store, or a professional practice, the principles are the same. Customers are searching differently. Platforms are evolving. Competition is increasing.

You do not have to fear AI.

But you cannot ignore it.

The businesses that adapt will stay visible. The ones that wait too long may struggle to catch up.

This guide is here to make sure you stay on the right side of that line.

Let's begin.

Chapter 1: Welcome to the Age of Intelligent Marketing

A Decade of Disruption

Every few years, marketing changes just enough to keep us on our toes. But recently, it has changed so completely that many professionals feel like they woke up in a different era, wondering, "How do I stay relevant in this modern age?" Artificial intelligence **(AI) has shifted** how businesses communicate, sell, and earn trust.

Search, content, and advertising used to follow predictable rules: type a keyword, write an ad, build a landing page. Today, machines predict intent before anyone clicks. They listen, learn, and sometimes respond faster than we can think. **We must understand how AI works, how to utilize it, and continually adapt as AI evolves.**

Why This Moment Feels Different

We've seen big shifts before: Web 2.0, the mobile revolution, the social boom, voice assistants, and video dominance. But this time, the change cuts across everything at once. AI-driven algorithms now not only rank information; they *create* it.

AI is shaping what people see, read, and believe. And, as a technology, its rate of growth, advancement, and adaptation is unprecedented.

It suggests what to buy, where to go, and which brands to trust. For a business owner, that means visibility no longer depends only on good content or smart ads. It depends on whether machines can understand your business well enough to recommend it.

From Search Bars to Conversations

Typing a keyword feels old-fashioned. Many users now talk to search engines instead of typing into them. They ask questions: "Who's the best electrician near me?" "What's the safest small SUV for families?" "How can I improve my Google ranking?"

Voice-based and conversational searches create sentences that look more like natural speech. Instead of a few high-volume keywords, we're dealing with thousands of unique, long questions every day. Each one reveals clear intent.

This new style of search rewards brands that publish clear, structured, human answers. The more your content mirrors how people speak, the more likely AI systems are to feature you in their results.

The Power Shift in Visibility

In traditional SEO, businesses competed for ten blue links on a results page. In modern AI search, there might be one summarized answer that combines information from several sources. That means fewer clicks, but higher rewards for those who earn inclusion.

Visibility today depends on *training* the AI to recognize you as a trusted authority. That involves clear branding, structured data, and consistent messaging across every digital channel. If the AI can't interpret who you are, it won't recommend you.

What "Invisible" Really Means

Being invisible no longer means you rank on page two of Google. It means you disappear entirely from the conversation. When customers ask a voice assistant for a service, the AI might mention one or two names. Everyone else vanishes.

Imagine the frustration of running a solid business but losing leads because an algorithm doesn't understand your content, address, or reputation signals. That's the risk many companies face right now.

How Small Businesses Can Still Win

Large corporations have deep budgets and in-house data teams. Small and midsize businesses can't outspend them, but they can out-adapt them. Flexibility and speed matter more than size.

Small companies can implement AI tools faster, personalize content better, and react to market changes in real time. They can publish authentic, expert-driven insights that large companies often struggle to replicate. In the AI era, agility beats bureaucracy.

Humans and Machines: The New Middle Ground

AI does the 'heavy lifting': processing data, automating tasks, and finding patterns. Humans provide the empathy, creativity, and strategy. The winning formula lies in cooperation, not competition.

Marketers who learn how to guide AI instead of fearing it will dominate the next decade. Those who ignore it may slowly fade from visibility, not because they failed, but because they weren't found.

Adapting Before You Have To

Every innovation cycle rewards early learners and early adopters. Businesses that experiment now with AI-driven SEO, predictive analytics, and automation will understand how to steer it later. Waiting until it's "the norm" means playing catch-up in a marketplace that moves faster every quarter.

The first step is awareness: know what's changing and why.

The second is action: start small, measure results, and grow with each iteration.

Takeaway Summary

- Artificial intelligence has become the backbone of modern marketing.

- AI's rate of growth, advancement, and adaptation is unprecedented.
- Visibility now depends on whether AI systems understand and trust your business.
- Conversational and voice searches create thousands of long-tail opportunities.
- Small businesses can win through agility, authenticity, and early adoption.
- The goal isn't to replace humans with machines, but to partner with them.

AI Tools to Explore

CHATGPT
- **(https://chat.openai.com):** conversational AI that helps with research, idea generation, and content drafting.

PERPLEXITY AI
- **(https://www.perplexity.ai):** a real-time conversational search engine that cites its sources.

GOOGLE GEMINI
- **(https://gemini.google.com):** Google's AI assistant that integrates with search, docs, and advertising tools.

CLAUDE AI

- **(https://claude.ai):** text-based AI with strong summarization and document-analysis features.

MIDJOURNEY

- **(https://www.midjourney.com):** a generative-image platform that produces brand visuals from text prompts.

Chapter 2: Search Evolved: From Keywords to Intelligence

A Brief History of Search Algorithms

Search used to be simple: type a keyword, get a list of results. Businesses tried to rank higher by stuffing those same keywords into titles, pages, and links. It worked for a while. Then Google started getting smarter.

RankBrain introduced machine learning. BERT taught search engines how to understand context. Now, AI models like Gemini and GPT Search process intent, tone, and meaning instead of just text. Search no longer reacts, it interprets.

How AI Changed the Meaning of Relevance

Old SEO focused on "matching words." Modern SEO focuses on "matching purpose." When someone searches for "how to fix a leaking pipe," they're not looking for a history lesson about plumbing. They want quick, trustworthy steps or a local plumber who can help.

AI reads between the lines. It weighs clarity, accuracy, and trust. It decides whether your content solves the problem completely. That's why relevance today means more than optimization. It means empathy.

Context Over Keywords

Search engines now analyze *entities*; people, places, brands, and topics; rather than exact phrases. This means your online reputation, reviews, and brand mentions all help define your "digital identity."

If someone asks, "Who's the best HVAC company near me?" AI doesn't just scan websites. It cross-references star ratings, proximity, and authority signals. It connects context from multiple data points to give a confident answer.

Semantic Search and Entity Recognition

Semantic search allows AI to link related meanings. It understands that "auto mechanic," "car repair shop," and "vehicle service center" can represent the same intent. That's why rigid keyword targeting feels outdated.

Marketers now focus on clusters of meaning instead of single terms. This creates depth and helps AI systems understand your expertise across multiple subjects.

Conversational Search Arrives

People talk to machines as if they were human: "What's the best email platform for small business?" or "Which type of solar panel lasts longest?" These are natural conversations, not typed commands.

AI interprets tone, phrasing, and implied needs. It looks for content that sounds conversational and helpful, not robotic. Writing as if you're speaking to someone across a desk is now good SEO practice.

Voice Search as the Ultimate Long-Tail Play

Voice search adds a new layer. When people speak, their questions get longer, more specific, and more personal. Instead of typing "plumber Austin," they'll say "Who can come fix a broken water heater in South Austin tonight?"

Each voice query becomes a unique long-tail keyword. Traditional SEO tools can't always track them, but conversational optimization; clear, well-structured answers; makes your site more discoverable.

Think of it this way: every voice query is a chance to connect directly with intent. You don't need to guess which keyword variation wins; you need to answer the question naturally and precisely.

Natural Language and the Death of Exact Match

Exact match keywords still have a role, especially for paid ads. But for organic ranking, natural language wins. When you write for humans first, AI understands your meaning better.

Search algorithms now use deep learning models to interpret context across entire pages. The result: relevance depends on how *clearly* you communicate, not how often you repeat phrases.

Intent-Driven Optimization in Plain English

To optimize for intent, start with this question: *What is the person behind the search trying to accomplish?*

If they want education, give them clarity. If they want to buy, make the next step obvious. If they want reassurance, show trust signals. Aligning content to real intent keeps AI engines confident in recommending you.

Zero-Click Search and What It Means for Visibility

Generative search engines often answer queries directly, which means fewer clicks. But when your content fuels those summaries, you still win. You may not get the click, but you gain brand exposure and authority.

Zero-click doesn't mean zero value. It means adapting your metrics: track mentions, impressions, and engagement from AI-generated responses. Visibility is still success, even if it looks different than it did in the past.

Human Content That AI Can Interpret

AI doesn't think like us; it reads patterns. So your content needs structure. Use clear headings, short paragraphs, and language that sounds natural. Label your sections logically, add schema markup, and use examples that clarify intent. The simpler your structure, the easier it is for AI to interpret and share your content. Writing for people and machines is no longer two separate goals; it's the same one.

Structure also helps AI understand hierarchy and context. When you organize ideas with consistent H1, H2, and H3 headings, bullet points, and concise sections, you signal what matters most and how topics relate to each other. That clarity makes it easier for search systems to extract answers, generate summaries, and surface your content in features like snippets or AI overviews. Walls of text or loosely organized pages force AI to guess, and when it has to guess, it often moves on to a competitor with cleaner formatting.

Specificity further improves interpretation. Clearly defined terms, direct answers, and concrete examples reduce ambiguity and help AI match your content to real user intent. Instead of vague statements, use precise language, step-by-step explanations, and descriptive labels.

Think of your page as structured data wrapped in readable prose: every heading, sentence, and element should make your meaning unmistakable. When your content is easy to parse, it becomes easier to recommend.

Takeaway Summary

- Search engines now understand meaning, not just words.
- AI-driven SEO focuses on intent, clarity, and reputation.
- Conversational and voice search create thousands of long-tail opportunities.
- Structured, natural language helps both people and machines understand your message.
- Visibility today depends on how well you communicate purpose, not just keywords.

AI Tools to Explore

GOOGLE SEARCH CONSOLE

- **(https://search.google.com/search-console):** monitor how Google interprets your website's structure and queries.

ALSOASKED

- **(https://alsoasked.com):** explore related conversational questions real users ask.

ANSWERTHEPUBLIC

- **(https://answerthepublic.com):** discover long-tail voice-style questions for content ideas.

CHATGPT

- **(https://chat.openai.com):** simulate conversational search and test how your content answers natural questions.

SEMRUSH

- **(https://www.semrush.com):** identify entity clusters, intent-based keywords, and ranking gaps.

Chapter 3: Generative Search and the Rise of GEO

What Is Generative Engine Optimization?

Generative Engine Optimization, or GEO, is the new frontier of search. It focuses on optimizing your visibility inside **AI-generated results** rather than the traditional list of links.

When people ask a question in Google's Search Generative Experience, or use conversational search engines like Perplexity and ChatGPT, they get an **AI-written summary**. That summary often blends information from multiple sources into one clean, human-sounding response.

The catch: if your business isn't part of the data that trains those responses, you don't exist in the conversation.

From Web Pages to AI Summaries

Generative search doesn't just index websites; it reads them, summarizes them, and paraphrases them into new sentences. That means your content needs to be *recognizable* to machines as high quality, trustworthy, and contextually relevant.

In the old days, SEO was about getting on page one. Today, it's about getting quoted by an algorithm. Your content should make it easy for AI to identify your expertise and re-use your information accurately.

Think of it this way: AI isn't reading your content like a person. It's scanning for patterns, structure, and context. The clearer those are, the better your chances of being featured in generated summaries.

How Google, ChatGPT, and Perplexity Pull Their Sources

Different AI engines pull data in different ways.

- **Google SGE** relies on web-crawled content, structured schema, and existing authority signals.
- **ChatGPT Search** (with its browsing features) looks for fresh, well-structured content that matches conversational intent.
- **Perplexity AI** prioritizes verifiable sources and clear author attribution.

All of them care about *trustworthiness*. That includes source credibility, factual accuracy, and domain authority. Sites that cite sources and demonstrate expertise are far more likely to appear in AI-generated outputs.

Content Depth vs. Surface-Level Answers

Shallow content doesn't perform well in generative search. AI systems reward pages that provide full explanations, definitions, and context. If your article answers only half a question, another source will fill in the rest; and may replace you.

Long-form, structured, and educational content performs best. It gives the AI enough data to understand your topic thoroughly. A single high-quality article can now outperform dozens of keyword-stuffed posts.

Training the Machine to Quote You

Every piece of content you publish is a training signal. When your site consistently uses clear phrasing, factual references, and helpful tone, AI systems learn that your material is reliable.

That reliability increases the odds of being cited in generated results. Include factual data, consistent branding, and author names where possible. Transparency helps both users and algorithms know you can be trusted.

On Consistent Branding

Consistent branding is about clearly stating who you are and what you do in language both people and machines understand. For example, "[Brand Name] is a roofing contractor in Austin, TX, specializing in hail damage repair". This kind of plain, explicit positioning helps AI systems accurately associate your business with specific services and locations. Rather than relying on inference, you're giving search engines direct, unambiguous context.

When your brand name, services, and location are presented consistently across your website, content, and listings, it reduces confusion and strengthens how your business is categorized in search systems. Over time, this consistency improves the chances that your brand is correctly represented in AI-generated answers, especially for local and service-based queries.

The goal isn't to "train" an AI in the machine-learning sense, but to make your identity machine-readable and difficult to misinterpret. Clarity creates credibility, and credibility is what earns inclusion in generative search results.

Authority Signals That Feed AI Responses

Generative engines look for more than text. They read your **metadata, reviews, backlinks, and citations**. The richer and more interconnected your presence, the more "weight" your content carries.

Authority comes from a combination of:

- **Reputation:** customer reviews, mentions, and testimonials.
- **Relevance:** consistent topics that build expertise over time.
- **Recency:** updated content that reflects current best practices.

This means that SEO, content, and reputation management now work together more closely than ever before.

Structured Data, Schema, and Citation Control

Schema markup is your direct line of communication with AI search. It helps systems categorize your pages correctly and know who authored them, what's being discussed, and which parts represent answers or products.

Adding schema to your pages can help AI engines "quote" the right section. It's like putting labels on every part of your website. Product schema, FAQ schema, and article schema are the most helpful for GEO.

Real-World Example: How One Article Became a Top AI Answer

A small roofing company published an article titled *How to Spot Hail Damage on Your Roof*. The article included clear step-by-step sections, real images, and a short FAQ with schema markup. Within a few weeks, Perplexity AI began citing the company as a source when users asked, "What does hail damage look like?"

No massive backlink campaign. No national exposure. Just well-structured, local expertise presented clearly. That's the power of GEO.

One article helped this roofing contractor gain recognition as a local expert in a highly profitable area of their business.

By the way, the fact that the company posted real images of roof damage was a key factor in the article's success. AI engines can perform reverse images searches in milliseconds and using stock photos can make a pro look like an amateur in a heartbeat.

AI needs to recognize you as legitimate before referring you to searchers.

Balancing Brand Voice with Machine Readability

AI optimization doesn't mean losing your personality. In fact, unique brand voice builds trust. The key is clarity over cleverness.

Write in a way that sounds human but still uses clear signals. Headings, lists, short sentences, and examples help AI interpret your meaning. Humor and storytelling are welcome, as long as they don't confuse structure.

Your brand should still feel authentic; it just needs to speak a language both people and machines understand.

Being Unique and Accurate

Being unique and accurate is no longer just good SEO hygiene. It is now a core requirement for visibility in an AI-driven search world. Modern search engines and AI systems don't simply match keywords anymore. They evaluate meaning, credibility, and originality. When dozens of competitors publish near-identical pages using the same templates, stock phrases, and recycled talking points, AI has no compelling reason to surface one over another. Generic content blends together and gets filtered out.

Unique content, on the other hand, gives AI distinctive signals to latch onto: original phrasing, specific examples, proprietary insights, real data, and first-hand experience. These elements help your page stand apart and increase the likelihood that AI systems select or quote your content as the best answer.

Accuracy matters just as much because AI models are designed to prioritize trust.

When you combine uniqueness with accuracy, you create content that is both memorable and dependable. That's exactly what AI systems are trying to deliver to users: the clearest, most trustworthy answer. Pages that provide original insight and factual clarity become easier for AI to extract, summarize, and recommend in featured snippets, AI overviews, and conversational search results.

In short, distinctive thinking earns attention, and precision earns trust. Together, they dramatically improve your odds of being chosen over the competition.

Takeaway Summary

- Generative search creates summaries, not just lists of links.
- GEO focuses on making your content easy for AI to cite, summarize, and trust.
- Clear structure, factual accuracy, and transparency increase your inclusion rate.
- Schema markup gives AI systems labels to understand your pages better.
- The goal isn't to game the machine; it's to help it represent you correctly.

- Authenticity matters in GEO. Using accurate yet unique language and real photos is one of the easiest ways to stand above the competition.

AI Tools to Explore

GOOGLE SEARCH GENERATIVE EXPERIENCE
- **(https://labs.google.com/search):** preview and test how Google's AI summaries present your brand.

PERPLEXITY AI
- **(https://www.perplexity.ai):** explore generative search results and see which sources are being cited.

SCHEMA.ORG
- **(https://schema.org):** the official library for structured data markup to help AI interpret your site.

YOAST SEO
- **(https://yoast.com):** WordPress plugin that simplifies schema implementation and readability improvements.

SURFERSEO
- **(https://surferseo.com):** content optimization platform that aligns page structure with AI-driven ranking factors.

Chapter 4: Answer Engines and the New SEO Frontier

Defining Answer Engine Optimization

Answer Engine Optimization, or AEO, is the art of helping AI-powered search engines find, understand, and quote your content when searchers ask their questions. Instead of competing for position on a list, you're competing for *inclusion in the answer itself*.

When someone asks an AI system, "What's the best CRM for small business?" the machine doesn't display 10 results; it synthesizes one summarized reply. The companies and sources inside that reply are the new winners.

Within Google, answers to People Also Ask (PAA) may be AI-generated when web content does not satisfy user's intent. When AI answers directly, fewer users click through to websites, potentially reducing organic traffic for sites.

AEO is SEO reimagined for this new environment. It's about giving AI exactly what it needs to speak confidently on your behalf **and utilizing opportunities to build more authoritative, complete answers to compete or get featured.**

From FAQ Pages to Conversational Content

Early AEO began with FAQ sections. You'd add "What is..." and "How do I..." questions with short answers. That still helps, but today's AI expects more depth.

Think of your website as a living knowledge base. Each article, guide, and video should answer real questions in clear language. Include reasoning, examples, and plain explanations; things an algorithm can pull without guessing context.

When AI detects direct, confident answers, it treats them as trustworthy data.

Voice Assistants & Smart Tech as Gatekeepers

Voice assistants have become the front line of search. Tools like Alexa, Siri, and Google Assistant now filter the internet for short, definitive answers.

When users say, "Hey Google, who installs water heaters near me?" or "Alexa, what's the best way to remove rust from steel?", those devices pull responses from sources with clear authority signals. The spoken format means fewer and more precise results; often, only one. That makes AEO the key to being heard when stop typing and start talking.

Writing for Natural Speech Patterns

Voice-based search prefers language that sounds like conversation. Avoid stiff phrasing. Use everyday wording, short sentences, and contractions when they fit naturally.

If you write like you talk, AI understands your tone better. Use question-based subheadings and direct responses below them. That helps search engines match the structure of natural Q&A.

For example:

Question: "How long does it take to install a new HVAC system?"
Answer: "Most installations take one to two days, depending on the size of your home and ductwork condition."

That clarity helps AI recognize and extract precise answers.

"Who," "What," and "How" as Ranking Triggers

Search engines often categorize intent using question words. "Who" signals people or businesses, "what" requests explanations, and "how" expects step-by-step solutions.

By naturally incorporating these question types into your content, you align with the way AI interprets user intent. It's not about forcing them in; it's about mirroring how real people ask.

Long-Tail Conversations and AI Memory

AI doesn't stop after one question. When someone follows up with "Why does that matter?" or "What's the cheapest option?", the system recalls the prior context.

That continuity means your content needs to be thorough enough to support ongoing dialogue. Think of each page as a self-contained micro-conversation that still fits within a larger topic cluster.

Long-tail queries, those ultra-specific questions, are the backbone of conversational search. Each represents a unique doorway to your brand.

Featured Snippets vs. AI Responses

Featured snippets were the old version of AEO. They showed one best answer at the top of Google results. Generative AI takes that further by blending multiple snippets and sources.

Your goal is still the same: earn trust by answering better, faster, and more completely than competitors. Snippet optimization; structured paragraphs, bullet points, and clear context; remains a key AEO skill.

Accuracy and Trust Signals in Voice Results

AI systems care deeply about credibility. They don't want to give wrong answers. If your data feels uncertain or outdated, you'll be excluded.

Always back claims with real examples or references. Use consistent facts across all channels; website, social media, and listings. Even small mismatches can make AI question your reliability.

Optimizing for Micro-Moments and Local Intention

Micro-moments are those brief bursts of curiosity when someone needs an instant answer: "nearest tire shop," "open late dentist," "best plumber for emergencies."

AI now predicts these before users even finish asking. By optimizing your listings, schema, and localized content, you can appear as the trusted solution in those moments.

AEO blends perfectly with **local SEO**: fast, accurate, and voice-friendly responses about real-world needs.

Integrating AEO into Your Existing SEO Playbook

AEO doesn't replace SEO; it expands it. Use your current optimization strategy as the foundation, then add layers for conversational and voice intent.

Update your pages with question-based headings, clean formatting, and structured data. **Reference Google's PAA for content opportunities.**

Review your analytics to see what queries already drive traffic. Turn those into more conversational answers.

Finally, test your own brand visibility by asking AI systems direct questions. See whether you appear in their replies.

Takeaway Summary

- AEO helps AI-powered engines find and quote your content directly.

- Voice assistants and conversational search drive new opportunities for discovery.
- Writing naturally and answering clearly makes your content easier for AI to reuse.
- Accuracy, local optimization, and trust signals define visibility in answer engines.
- AEO complements SEO; it doesn't replace it.

AI Tools to Explore

- **AnswerThePublic**
- **(https://answerthepublic.com):** find real user questions to inspire AEO-friendly content.
- **AlsoAsked**
- **(https://alsoasked.com):** map follow-up questions users ask in conversational search.
- **Google's People Also Ask** (built into search results): insight into common Q&A opportunities.
- **ChatGPT**
- **(https://chat.openai.com):** test how AI interprets and summarizes your answers quickly.
- **Schema Markup Validator**
- **(https://validator.schema.org):** confirm that your FAQ and article schema are readable to AI systems.

Chapter 5: Paid Media in the AI Age

How AI Rewrote the Ad Auction

There was a time when advertisers spent hours adjusting bids by hand. You'd watch click costs rise and fall, move budgets around, and hope you made the right call. Those days are mostly gone.

Today, AI runs the auction. It monitors billions of signals; time of day, device, search intent, user behavior; and places bids automatically. It predicts who will convert before the user even clicks.

For marketers, that means less manual control but more precision. The algorithms do the math faster and smarter than any human could. Our role has shifted from adjusting numbers to guiding strategy.

Performance Max and Smart Bidding Explained

Google's Performance Max campaigns combine multiple ad formats; Search, Display, YouTube, Maps, and Discover; into one unified system. AI allocates budget where it predicts the best outcomes.

Smart Bidding uses the same principle. Instead of one static cost per click, AI calculates value per impression. It considers location, device, intent, and past conversion patterns. Over time, it learns what's most likely to produce a profitable lead.

This is not guesswork. It's pattern recognition at scale.

Local Services Ads and AI Trust Metrics

Local Services Ads (LSAs) now use AI to measure credibility. They factor in reviews, response time, and proximity. When users say, "Find an HVAC repair company near me," Google decides which businesses seem most reliable.

That reliability score; part performance, part trust; determines visibility. The higher your reputation metrics, the more often you appear. AI-driven trust signals now matter as much as budget.

Predictive Budget Allocation

AI doesn't wait until the end of the month to show you results. It adjusts in real time. If a campaign underperforms, the system instantly reallocates funds toward better-converting audiences.

That means budgets behave dynamically: they expand or contract based on results. For agencies and small businesses, this creates new opportunities for efficiency. You can reach the same audience with less waste.

Creative Testing Without Manual A/B Work

In the past, you'd test headlines and images one by one. Now AI runs thousands of combinations simultaneously. Responsive Search Ads, for example, rotate variations automatically and keep the best performers.

The system doesn't just count clicks; it analyzes engagement quality. It learns which tone, image, or call-to-action connects best with each audience segment.

The marketer's job is to feed it strong creative options and clear goals. The AI does the rest.

AI Forecasting Conversions Before They Happen

Modern ad platforms use predictive modeling to estimate which users will convert next. They factor in user history, intent signals, and demographic behavior.

For example, Meta's Advantage+ campaigns predict which ad placement will drive sales even before launch. Google's Smart Bidding anticipates future conversions based on recent data.

The result: campaigns that self-optimize while running.

Human Oversight in Automated Ad Campaigns

AI may handle mechanics, but it doesn't know your brand's story. That's where humans come in. We interpret performance beyond numbers; understanding tone, reputation, and emotional response.

Automation works best when humans set clear guardrails. Without oversight, algorithms can over-target, overspend, or drift toward the wrong audience. Your judgment keeps the system aligned with business goals.

The Myth of "Set and Forget" Automation

Automation does not mean autopilot. Successful campaigns still need creative refreshes, audience review, and ongoing optimization.

AI learns from the data you feed it. If that data goes stale, your performance will too. Treat automation as a partnership: you provide fresh input, the system provides constant learning.

Real-World Examples of ROI Shifts

A plumbing company switched from manual keyword bidding to Performance Max. Their cost per lead dropped by 25 percent within six weeks.

A national e-commerce brand moved its product ads into Google's predictive campaign model. Click-through rates rose 40 percent, but more importantly, return on ad spend improved by nearly 60 percent.

The takeaway: AI's efficiency compounds over time when paired with consistent human direction.

Balancing Data and Gut Instinct

Data tells you what's happening. Intuition tells you why. Combining both creates the best results.

AI might recommend more budget toward one audience, but if you know that audience is seasonally inconsistent, you can override it. Numbers alone can't capture local nuance, brand tone, or community reputation.

Human instinct remains the final filter.

Takeaway Summary

- AI now manages bids, budgets, and creative testing automatically.

- Success depends on clear goals, consistent data, and active human oversight.

- Reputation metrics, reviews, and responsiveness heavily influence Local Services Ads.

- Predictive automation cuts waste but still needs fresh creative input.

- Balance data with intuition to stay both efficient and authentic.

AI Tools to Explore

GOOGLE ADS PERFORMANCE MAX

- **(https://ads.google.com):** unified campaign type using AI to manage placements and bids.

META ADVANTAGE+

- **(https://www.facebook.com/business/advantage-plus):** predictive ad platform optimizing delivery and audience selection.

MICROSOFT ADVERTISING AUTOMATION

- **(https://about.ads.microsoft.com):** smart bidding and responsive ad tools for Bing and LinkedIn networks.

OPTMYZR

- **(https://www.optmyzr.com):** AI-powered PPC management software that gives you human-level control over automation.

ADCREATIVE.AI

- **(https://www.adcreative.ai):** generates headlines and visuals based on brand and audience data for rapid creative testing.

Chapter 6: The Creative Revolution: Design, Video, and Branding in the AI Era

The Role of Designers in an Automated World

AI is changing what it means to be a designer. Tasks that once took hours can now be handled in less time with AI tools.

The designer's role is evolving from executor to strategist. Instead of just creating assets, designers are now able to focus on creative vision and think about experience, storytelling, ethics, accessibility, and emotional impact.

AI handles the manual, repetitive work allowing designers to implement meaningful, human-centered design with photos, websites, imagery, video, and creative data.

From Stock Art to Synthetic Art

Not long ago, designers relied on stock photo libraries and hours of manual editing. Now, AI tools can create custom visuals from a single sentence. You can describe an image in words, and the system paints it instantly.

This shift is redefining creative production forever. The cost of testing visual ideas has dropped to almost zero. Teams can explore ten design directions before breakfast. Creativity is no longer limited by time or technical skill.

How Tools Like Midjourney and Runway Changed Design Speed

Midjourney and Runway have become the new creative accelerators. They allow designers to produce illustrations, backgrounds, and motion graphics in seconds.

Marketers can now visualize campaign ideas instantly. Instead of waiting days for mockups, teams can generate concepts in minutes and refine the best ones. The speed of experimentation encourages boldness.

Note: When production barriers disappear, imagination expands.

Visual Branding in the Age of Infinite Variation

One challenge of AI-generated design is consistency. With endless options, it's easy to lose brand identity. AI can mimic styles, but it can also wander into visual noise.

The solution is to train AI systems on your own brand assets. Upload color palettes, logo examples, typography, and reference imagery. Many tools now let you build custom "style models" that keep outputs on brand.

A brand's strength in the AI era comes from *clarity of identity*. The clearer your visual rules, the easier it is to stay recognizable in a sea of content.

Prompt Design as the New Creative Skill

Prompt design has become the new form of art direction. How you describe your idea determines the outcome. Small word changes create massive visual differences.

Learning how to craft specific, layered prompts is essential. Instead of saying "a modern kitchen," say "a bright, stainless-steel kitchen with natural sunlight and minimalist decor." That extra context gives the AI a creative compass.

Prompt writing blends creativity with precision. It's not about knowing code; it's about knowing how to clearly communicate your vision.

Ethics and Copyright in AI Imagery

AI-generated images raise tough questions about ownership. Who owns an image created by a machine trained on millions of existing works? Laws continue to evolve, but businesses should act cautiously.

Always disclose when you use AI-generated visuals. Avoid prompts that reference specific artists or brands. When in doubt, combine AI creativity with human editing to ensure originality.

Transparency protects your reputation and builds trust with your audience.

AI Video Generation and Storytelling

Video has become the centerpiece of modern marketing. AI tools like Runway, Pika, and Synthesia can now generate full video scenes from text or images.

This opens the door for small businesses that couldn't afford video production before. You can script, voice, and animate promotional content without cameras or studios.

Still, storytelling remains the human edge. AI can animate visuals, but only you can shape a story that connects emotionally.

Human Emotion as a Design Advantage

AI can replicate visual style, but not emotional depth. People instinctively recognize authenticity. A photo of a real team member will always feel warmer than a synthetic face.

Use AI for scale, variation, and experimentation. But balance it with real people, stories, and expression. Authenticity anchors your brand in trust.

Creativity that blends emotion and technology feels modern, innovative, and human.

Combining Data and Aesthetics to Achieve Higher Engagement

AI gives creatives data they never had before. Platforms like Canva's Magic Studio and Adobe Sensei analyze how users respond to different colors, fonts, and layouts.

This feedback helps designers refine visuals based on audience behavior. It bridges the gap between art and analytics. When design choices are guided by both emotion and evidence, engagement naturally improves.

Curating AI Outputs for Brand Consistency

AI produces many options, but quantity is not quality. Curation is the new creative discipline. The best designers are becoming editors who select and refine AI output.

Establish review checkpoints in your workflow. Look for alignment with tone, clarity, and message. Remember that AI can assist, but it can't judge. You decide what's right for your audience.

How to Integrate AI into Your Creative Team

Start by introducing AI tools for brainstorming and concepting. Use them to accelerate drafts, not replace creative staff.

Train your team to think of AI as a collaborator. Set clear roles. AI creates options, and the humans select, polish, and finalize. This mindset keeps control where it belongs, with the people who understand your brand best. Free your team to focus on strategy, storytelling, and vision.

The most creative teams in 2026 will be those that master collaboration between human imagination and artificial intelligence. Teams that embrace AI as a collaborator, not a replacement, will move more efficiently, innovate more freely, and maintain authentic branding.

Takeaway Summary

- AI allows anyone to create high-quality visuals and videos quickly.
- Prompt writing is now a critical creative skill.
- Brand consistency depends on guiding AI with clear identity rules.

- Ethics, originality, and disclosure matter as much as design quality.
- Human emotion and judgment remain irreplaceable in creative work.

AI Tools to Explore

MIDJOURNEY
- **(https://www.midjourney.com):** generates custom illustrations, concept art, and brand imagery from text prompts.

RUNWAY ML
- **(https://runwayml.com):** quickly creates AI-powered video scenes, edits footage, and removes backgrounds automatically.

ADOBE FIREFLY
- **(www.adobe.com/products/firefly.html):** easily integrates AI-generated visuals within Photoshop and Illustrator.

CANVA MAGIC STUDIO
- **(https://www.canva.com/magic/):** design generation and layouts based on engagement data.

PIKA LABS
- **(https://pika.art):** easily turns still images or short prompts into animated video clips.

Chapter 7: Content Creation in the Age of Machines

The AI Writer as Your Co-Author

Artificial intelligence has become the new writing partner for marketers, copywriters, and entrepreneurs. You can ask an AI to draft a blog, summarize research, or create ad copy in seconds. What once took hours now takes minutes.

But speed is not the goal. Clarity, originality, and trust are. AI can generate words, but it relies on your direction to give them purpose. The best results come from treating AI as a co-author, not a ghostwriter.

You bring the insight. The AI brings the acceleration.

Two Categories of AI

Not all AI do the same job. In content creation, there are two main categories worth understanding: **assistive AI** and **generative AI**.

Assistive AI helps you **improve** what already exists. These tools work to correct grammar, enhance clarity, flag inconsistencies, and optimize readability. These tools offer similar abilities as spellcheck, grammar suggestions, tone analysis, or SEO optimization tools. They don't create content from scratch, but they can sharpen what you've written. Assistive AI is about refinement and quality control.

Generative AI, on the other hand, **does create** content. It can produce drafts, outlines, headlines, summaries, and full articles from prompts. This is the category most people think of when they hear "AI writing." Generative AI is powerful, but it requires strong direction and careful editing. Left alone, it can produce technically fluent but shallow, emotionless content.

Understanding the difference matters. Assistive AI is your editor. Generative AI is your junior writer. Both can save time, but neither replaces human judgment and tone.

Prompt Engineering 101 for Marketers

Every AI draft begins with a prompt. The clearer your instructions, the better the outcome. Think of it like briefing a junior writer: you must explain tone, audience, and purpose.

A weak prompt gives you filler. A strong prompt gives you focus. Instead of typing "write a blog on HVAC maintenance," try "write a friendly, 600-word blog explaining three simple ways homeowners can maintain their HVAC systems before summer, using plain conversational English and a helpful tone."

AI follows your lead. Be detailed, but natural. The more context you give, the more human the writing feels. You can also ask AI to customize your output to avoid the most common AI indicators. Try adding this to your prompt: "Emulate human writing styles and avoid **stylistic tells**, including punctuation habits such as Em dashes (—) and overly consistent sentence and paragraph length." But more on this in a moment under "A Look at Common AI Trends to Watch Out For."

Structuring Content That AI & Humans Both Love

AI models prefer structure: clear headings, logical flow, and short sentences. Humans prefer the same. That's good news.

Break long paragraphs into digestible sections. Use question-style subheadings. Present lists or short summaries for key takeaways.

This structure helps readers scan quickly and also helps AI identify your page as well-organized, improving visibility in generative search results.

Voice Search and Conversational Copywriting

Voice and conversational search have changed how people discover written content. Readers are now *listeners*.

Your copy should sound like spoken conversation: simple, direct, and natural. Use contractions, keep sentences short, and imagine someone hearing your words aloud.

For example, "Our team offers full-service plumbing solutions" sounds polished but formal. "We fix leaks, replace pipes, and handle every plumbing problem you can imagine" sounds conversational.

If it sounds good out loud, it's good for AI too.

Maintaining Tone and Brand Authenticity

AI can mimic tone, but it doesn't understand your brand's story. That's your job. Before using AI, define your voice: serious, casual, witty, or professional.

When you edit AI drafts, look for authenticity. Replace generic phrases with real experiences or brand-specific language. Consistency builds trust. Readers can tell when content feels genuine.

The goal is not to make AI sound human; it's to make it sound like *you*.

Editorial Oversight and Human Editing for AI Drafts

AI can generate strong first drafts but weak final drafts. Human editing remains essential. Always review for accuracy, tone, and logic.

Check facts, sources, and phrasing. Replace vague statements with specific ones. Add examples that reflect your real-world knowledge.

Editing transforms AI text into professional writing. It's where your expertise turns machine output into meaningful communication.

Content Layering: Depth Over Quantity

Old SEO favored volume. The more articles you posted, the better your chances of ranking. Today, AI favors *depth*.

It values complete, trustworthy coverage of a topic. One in-depth guide now outperforms ten short posts. Quality beats quantity every time.

Think of your website as a library. Each page should answer one key question thoroughly and clearly. That approach builds authority in the eyes of both humans and machines.

Repurposing AI-Generated Assets Across Formats

AI makes content recycling easier than ever. A single blog can become a video script, social post, or email sequence with just a few edits.

You can use one prompt to create multiple assets: blog summaries, infographics, or captions. This saves time while keeping your messaging consistent across platforms.

Repurposing isn't repetition; it's amplification.

Detecting and Fixing AI Hallucinations

AI sometimes invents facts or statistics. This problem is known as "hallucination." It happens when the model fills in gaps with assumptions.

Always verify data from external sources. Never publish numbers or quotes without checking. Fact-checking protects your credibility and keeps your content legally safe.

AI is smart, but it doesn't know truth; it knows patterns. That's why human review is non-negotiable.

A Look at Common AI Trends to Watch Out For

AI content has style patterns, and once you know them, you'll start seeing them everywhere. Some are harmless. Others slowly damage credibility if left unedited.

One common issue is **repetitive phrasing**. AI tends to re-use sentence structures, favorite transitions, and familiar expressions. If you see the same rhythm over and over, real editing and tone adjustment can break it up.

Another giveaway is the **overuse of the em dash**: "—" a stylistic choice that appears in many AI-generated drafts. There's nothing wrong with an occasional use of the dash, but when it begins to show up in every paragraph it can come across as disingenuous or redundant.

Then there's what marketers often call **"hype speak."** This includes exaggerated claims and inflated language such as:

- "It's not big.. It's HUGE."
- "This will change everything."
- "The ultimate solution you've been waiting for."

AI's preference of intensity and emphasis can disrupt your overall tone and make your content feel less "human" to your audience.

None of these issues mean AI is bad. They simply mean it needs human supervision. The best AI content will be the kind that was edited, polished, and refined by a human touch.

Perfecting the Prompt

Let's combine what we know about developing the ideal prompt to get good, clear, accurate content via AI without making it obvious that AI was used.

"Using a conversational plain-English writing style, create a reader-friendly, 600-word blog explaining three simple ways homeowners can maintain their HVAC systems before summer. Avoid stylistic tells such as Em dashes (—) and overly consistent sentence and paragraph length. Do not use repetitive phrasing, hype speak, or exaggerated claims. Also cite all sources when quotes, references, and/ or statistics are used."

You can reuse that exact prompt for every writing assignment by simply swapping out the document length and subject. However, it's best to customize this to your writing style by making constant tweaks to the prompt until it feels most like your voice.

When to Use AI and When to Write It Yourself

AI excels at drafting outlines, headlines, and short-form content. It struggles with deep storytelling or emotion.

Use AI for structure and speed. Write it yourself when emotion or trust matters most. This typically includes emails, mission statements, or personal stories.

A balanced workflow combines AI's efficiency with your human judgment.

Takeaway Summary

- Treat AI as a co-author, not a replacement.
- Strong prompts create focused, useful writing.
- Always fact-check and edit AI drafts for tone.
- Combine AI speed with human authenticity.

AI Tools to Explore

CHATGPT
- **(https://chat.openai.com):** generates text drafts, headlines, outlines, and dialogue for content.

JASPER
- **(https://www.jasper.ai):** AI writing assistant tailored for marketing, sales, and blog content.

GRAMMARLY
- **(https://www.grammarly.com):** proofreads grammar, tone, and clarity in AI or human-written text.

COPY.AI
- **(https://www.copy.ai):** produces ad copy, blog intros, and marketing text from short prompts.

QUILLBOT
- **(https://quillbot.com):** rephrases and refines content to improve readability and originality.

Chapter 8: Social Media: Where AI Meets Emotion

Algorithms That Know You Better Than You Do

Social media has become a mirror that knows what we like before we do. Every scroll, like, and pause sends a signal. AI algorithms use these signals to decide what we see next.

That means your feed isn't random; it's a prediction engine built to keep you engaged. It learns your habits, your mood, and even your curiosity. For marketers, this creates both opportunity and responsibility.

The challenge is no longer reaching people; it's connecting in ways that feel human in a machine-driven environment.

How AI Predicts Viral Content

AI tools can now analyze past posts and predict what will go viral. They measure tone, timing, hashtags, and even color palettes. Platforms like TikTok and Instagram rely heavily on machine learning to surface high-engagement content.

But virality isn't luck anymore. It's pattern recognition. AI identifies common emotional triggers; humor, surprise, nostalgia; and rewards them with exposure.

If you want to reach people organically, create content that taps into emotion, not just information. AI pushes posts that make people *feel*.

Social Listening and Sentiment Analysis

AI-powered listening tools monitor public conversations about brands, topics, and trends. They analyze tone: positive, negative, or neutral.

This allows companies to understand how people feel in real time. Instead of reacting late, you can adjust your messaging immediately.

For example, if customers complain about response time, you'll know within hours. If a campaign sparks excitement, you can double down quickly.

Social listening turns feedback into foresight.

Conversational AI in Customer Engagement

Many businesses now use chatbots to manage social messages and comments. The newest AI chat systems can respond naturally, with empathy and context.

When done right, these systems save time and build trust. They answer FAQs instantly and route complex issues to real humans. The secret is balance; automation for speed, humans for understanding.

Never let convenience replace connection. People still value real voices behind the brand.

AI-Generated Reels, Shorts, and Posts

AI has entered creative production on social media. You can now generate short videos, captions, and hashtags automatically. Tools can analyze trending sounds and match your visuals to them.

For small teams, this is a breakthrough. It means you can compete with larger brands without massive budgets. But remember: automation should serve storytelling, not replace it.

Even the most polished AI-generated clip falls flat without personality.

The Rise of Chatbots That Sound Like People

AI can mimic conversational tone so closely that users sometimes forget they're chatting with software. These chatbots can recommend products, book appointments, or follow up with leads.

Used ethically, this enhances customer experience. Used carelessly, it can feel deceptive. Always disclose automation, and offer a way to reach a human. Transparency strengthens trust.

Timing and Frequency: AI's Predictive Scheduling

AI tools can analyze when your audience is most active and predict the ideal times to post. They adjust frequency based on engagement trends, holidays, or audience fatigue.

This turns guesswork into strategy. You no longer need to rely on trial and error. AI's timing helps ensure your posts land when people actually want to see them.

But remember, consistency still matters more than perfection. A predictable rhythm builds familiarity.

Community Building With Authentic Responses

AI can help manage volume, but it can't build community. True engagement comes from real interaction; thanking followers, replying thoughtfully, and showing personality.

Audiences can tell the difference between a reply written by a person and one generated automatically. Use AI to lighten your workload, not to replace your presence.

Every authentic response adds a layer of loyalty.

Ethical Boundaries in AI Influencer Marketing

AI-generated influencers and avatars are on the rise. They look real, act real, and sometimes attract millions of followers.

This new world raises questions about transparency and authenticity. Should audiences know when a person isn't real? The answer is yes. Clear disclosure maintains credibility.

Real or virtual, trust still drives influence.

From Metrics to Meaning: Humanizing Data

AI provides detailed analytics; engagement rates, impressions, click-throughs; but the real story lies beneath the numbers.

A post that gets fewer likes might still change minds. A video with moderate views might build long-term relationships.

Human interpretation gives data its purpose. AI measures quantity. You measure quality.

Takeaway Summary

- AI predicts what content we see, share, and respond to.
- Emotional connection drives visibility more than technical precision.
- Chatbots and automation improve speed, but humans build trust.
- Predictive posting helps with timing, but consistency matters most.
- Data without empathy is empty; combine both for lasting impact.

AI Tools to Explore

HOOTSUITE OWLYWRITER AI

- **(https://www.hootsuite.com):** generates captions, hashtags, and posting schedules using AI analysis.

LATELY AI
- **(https://www.lately.ai):** turns long-form content into social media posts that match your brand voice.

BRANDWATCH
- **(https://www.brandwatch.com):** monitors public conversations and sentiment across social platforms.

MANYCHAT
- **(https://manychat.com):** automates conversations on Facebook, Instagram, and WhatsApp.

PREDIS.AI
- **(https://predis.ai):** creates complete post layouts, captions, and visuals with AI-driven audience insights.

Chapter 9: Predictive Analytics and Personalization

What Predictive Analytics Really Means

Predictive analytics is the science of looking forward using what we already know. It studies patterns in customer behavior to forecast what might happen next.

Every purchase, click, or abandoned cart becomes a clue. AI reads those clues, finds trends, and turns them into predictions. This helps businesses plan smarter; who to target, what to offer, and when to deliver it.

Think of it as marketing's weather forecast: not perfect, but accurate enough to prepare for what's coming.

Machine Learning & Behavioral Modeling in Action

Machine learning analyzes massive amounts of customer data. It groups users by behavior instead of demographics. For example, it can find patterns among people who buy at midnight, those who only shop on mobile, or those who always click sale links.

These insights guide campaign timing, ad spend, and product recommendations. The system keeps learning every time someone interacts with your brand.

It's personalization that grows smarter with every touch.

How AI Anticipates Customer Needs

Predictive models help brands meet needs before customers even speak them. A streaming platform might recommend a movie right when you're most likely to relax. An online retailer might send an offer for shoes that match the jacket you just bought.

AI anticipates timing and context. It connects behavior with opportunity. For small businesses, this means turning casual visitors into loyal customers through subtle, well-timed engagement.

Voice Data as a Goldmine for Intent Insights

Voice search adds a new dimension to prediction. Spoken queries reveal emotion, urgency, and context that text searches don't. When someone says "Where can I find a**n emergency HVAC technician** right now?", that urgency tells the system exactly what to prioritize.

AI tools that process voice data can identify patterns in tone and phrasing. Over time, they learn which types of questions lead to sales, support calls, or product interest.

Understanding how people *speak* helps you anticipate what they'll *need*.

Building Profiles Without Third-Party Cookies

Privacy laws and browser updates have made third-party cookies unreliable. AI now helps marketers shift toward first-party data; information users willingly share.

Predictive tools can analyze that data to fill the gaps cookies once covered. They look at purchase history, email engagement, and on-site behavior to create complete customer profiles without invading privacy.

This approach keeps personalization strong and ethical.

First-Party Data and Ethical Collection

The foundation of modern marketing is trust. Always be transparent about what data you collect and how you use it. Offer value in return, such as discounts, insights, or convenience.

When customers understand the benefit, they're more willing to share accurate information. Ethical data practices build loyalty that no algorithm can fake.

Dynamic Personalization Across Channels

Predictive personalization works best when every channel is connected. A customer who browses your website should see consistent messages in email and social ads.

AI platforms can track user journeys in real time. They update recommendations instantly based on new actions. This creates smooth, personalized experiences that feel natural, not intrusive.

Personalization isn't about showing different people different ads. It's about showing the *right* message to each person at the right time.

Automation That Still Feels Personal

AI can automate outreach without sounding robotic. Dynamic content lets emails and ads adapt to individual interests. For example, two users might receive the same newsletter, but each sees product images tailored to their browsing history.

The secret is tone. Write naturally, like a human speaking to another human. Let the AI handle timing and structure, but always shape the voice yourself.

Automation should enhance empathy, not erase it.

The New Privacy Playbook: Transparency & Trust

Privacy concerns continue to grow. Regulators now hold companies accountable for misuse of data. AI tools can actually help by enforcing compliance automatically.

Modern analytics systems can flag risky data, anonymize sensitive information, and manage consent. Transparency isn't just the right thing; it's a competitive advantage.

When people trust you with their data, they trust you with their business.

Using Predictive Insights to Drive Real Decisions

Prediction only matters if it leads to action. AI analytics should guide your business strategy, not just fill dashboards.

Use insights to adjust offers, update pricing, or refine targeting. Watch how predictive models evolve, and review outcomes regularly. AI gives you the roadmap, but you still have to steer.

Human judgment makes predictions practical.

Takeaway Summary

- Predictive analytics turns past behavior into future opportunity.
- Machine learning identifies intent faster and more accurately than manual analysis.
- Voice search reveals emotional context and urgency.
- First-party data and transparency replace old cookie tracking methods.
- Real personalization balances automation with human empathy.

AI Tools to Explore

HUBSPOT AI

- **(https://www.hubspot.com):** analyzes customer data to automate personalized campaigns across email and web.

GOOGLE ANALYTICS 4 (GA4)

- **(https://analytics.google.com):** uses predictive metrics to identify likely purchasers and churn risk.

SEGMENT
- **(https://segment.com):** consolidates first-party data and builds real-time customer profiles for personalization.

PEGA CUSTOMER DECISION HUB
- **(https://www.pega.com):** delivers predictive recommendations across customer touchpoints.

LEVITY AI
- **(https://levity.ai):** automates tagging, categorization, and behavioral modeling without coding.

Chapter 10: The Human Advantage: Where Machines Still Need Us

Why Empathy Can't Be Automated

Artificial intelligence can analyze tone and behavior, but it doesn't *feel* what people feel. It can predict what a customer might want, but it can't understand **why** the customer wants it.

Empathy builds trust. It's what makes a brand sound genuine, not scripted. When a customer is frustrated, an empathetic response turns a problem into loyalty. No algorithm can replace that human connection.

Creative Instinct vs. Algorithmic Logic

AI follows data patterns. Humans follow inspiration. A campaign that breaks rules often works precisely because it's unexpected.

AI recommends what's "likely to succeed." Humans create what no one has seen yet. That spark of originality, such as an odd headline, a bold visual, or an emotional twist, keeps marketing alive. Creativity begins where predictability ends.

Building Trust Through Storytelling

Stories move people in ways that data can't. A graph might prove success, but a story makes it memorable.

Share the human side of your business: why you started, what challenges you overcame, what you believe in. Stories connect customers to values, not just products. AI can summarize facts, but it can't feel purpose.

Human Touchpoints in Automated Journeys

Automation streamlines marketing, but human touchpoints give it soul. A personal thank-you note after a purchase, a quick phone call, or a handwritten card stands out in an automated world.

Customers remember kindness more than speed. Technology should make space for human gestures, not replace them.

Leadership in the AI Transition

AI changes tools, but leadership changes culture. Teams need guidance to adapt, experiment, and stay grounded.

A good leader sets direction, explains why AI matters, and ensures people don't feel replaced. Empower employees to use AI confidently and creatively. The best leaders help teams evolve without losing heart.

Upskilling Your Team for Hybrid Workflows

Tomorrow's marketers will blend technology fluency with emotional intelligence. Train teams to use AI tools effectively and to question their results.

Encourage learning in small doses: quick tutorials, sandbox projects, or peer-to-peer demos. Skill growth keeps curiosity alive and fear low. Knowledge builds confidence, and confidence fuels creativity.

The Emotional Side of Adoption and Change

Change often feels like loss. People worry that automation means replacement.

Leaders must address that emotion honestly. AI doesn't eliminate people; it eliminates tasks that drain them. When teams see that, they embrace technology rather than resist it.

Turning Fear of AI into Curiosity

Curiosity is the antidote to fear. Encourage your team to ask, "What else can this tool do?" instead of "What if this replaces me?"

Set up internal challenges or creative sprints using AI. When people explore freely, they discover value for themselves.

Curiosity transforms anxiety into innovation.

Culture as a Competitive Edge

Culture is the one advantage AI can't copy. It's built through trust, collaboration, and shared purpose.

Companies that value learning, openness, and respect will attract both talent and customers. In the long run, emotional intelligence outperforms automation. A healthy culture keeps technology human.

Re-Humanizing Marketing Before It's Too Late

As AI takes over analytics, bidding, and automation, marketing risks losing its warmth. The solution is balance: technology for precision, humanity for meaning. Let AI handle repetitive work so you can focus on empathy, storytelling, and creativity. The future belongs to brands that remember people come first.

Automation can optimize bids, forecast trends, and process mountains of data faster than any team ever could. That efficiency is valuable, but it also creates a temptation to treat marketing like a math problem instead of a relationship. When every decision is driven only by dashboards and algorithms, messaging starts to feel transactional and interchangeable. Customers notice. Ads sound the same. Emails feel robotic. Brands begin to blur together. Performance may hold steady for a while, but loyalty quietly erodes because nothing feels personal or memorable.

This is where human judgment matters most. Strategy, positioning, and voice cannot be automated without losing nuance. People connect with stories, shared frustrations, humor, and authenticity. They respond to brands that sound like real humans solving real problems. Empathy turns data into insight. Creativity turns insight into connection. AI can tell you what happened and even predict what might happen next, but it can't genuinely understand why something matters to your audience or how it feels to live their experience. That gap is where human marketers create value.

The smartest approach is not replacing people with machines, but redesigning roles so each does what it does best. Let AI handle the repetitive work: reporting, testing variations, adjusting bids, tagging audiences, and crunching numbers. Free your team to focus on conversations, ideas, and experiences that technology cannot replicate. When automation supports humanity instead of replacing it, marketing becomes both more efficient and more meaningful. In the long run, the brands that win won't be the most automated. They'll be the ones that still feel human.

Takeaway Summary

- Empathy, creativity, and storytelling keep brands human and relatable.
- AI assists logic. Humans bring intuition and originality, keeping the experience real.
- Leadership and culture help to drive successful AI adoption.
- Upskilling turns fear into confidence.
- The strongest marketing combines automation with heart.

AI Tools to Explore

NOTION AI
- **(https://www.notion.so/product/ai):** excels at helping teams brainstorm, summarize meetings, and document creative ideas.

MIRO
- **(https://miro.com):** collaborative whiteboard for mapping hybrid workflows and AI integration plans.

OTTER.AI
- **(https://otter.ai):** transcribes and summarizes meetings so teams can focus on discussion, not note-taking.

GOOGLE WORKSPACE AI FEATURES
- **(https://workspace.google.com):** integrates AI assistance across Docs, Sheets, and Gmail for collaboration.

TRELLO WITH BUTLER AUTOMATION
- **(https://trello.com):** helps automate simple tasks while keeping team workflows transparent and human-centered.

Chapter 11: Building Your AI-Ready Marketing Strategy

Assessing Your Current AI Readiness

Before you adopt new tools, you need to know where you stand today. Look at how your team currently manages marketing, including content creation, ads, analytics, and communication. There are many places where AI can help, but many more where it is not yet the solution.

Ask simple questions:

- What tasks take the most time?
- Where do errors or delays happen?
- Which areas depend heavily on guesswork?

AI works best when it fills gaps, not when it's added for the sake of novelty. Identify one or two areas where automation can make an immediate difference.

Auditing Tools and Platforms You Already Use

Many businesses already use AI without realizing it. Google Ads, social platforms, and analytics dashboards all rely on machine learning.

Audit your existing systems. See which features include AI assistance and whether your team uses them fully. Sometimes, the fastest way to improve isn't adding new tools; it's mastering the ones you already have.

Creating a Cross-Channel AI Integration Plan

AI delivers the best results when your channels work together. Your website, ads, social media, and email campaigns should share the same data foundation.

Build a simple integration map that shows where data flows and where it stops. If one platform can't talk to another, find connectors or automation tools to bridge the gap. When systems share insights, AI can personalize and predict more effectively.

Budgeting for Technology and Training

AI tools range from free to enterprise-level investments. Start small, test results, and scale only what works.

Allocate budget not just for software, but also for training. A well-trained team delivers more value than an expensive platform used poorly.

Think of AI as an employee; it needs onboarding, maintenance, and review.

Defining KPIs for AI-Assisted Performance

Set measurable goals. AI is powerful, but without metrics, it's directionless.

KPIs might include reduced cost per lead, faster content creation, improved engagement, or higher conversion rates. Track results weekly or monthly and look for consistent patterns, not one-time spikes.

Let data confirm that AI is improving performance, not just adding activity.

Choosing the Right Partners and Vendors

Evaluate AI vendors the same way you evaluate employees: check credibility, transparency, and compatibility.

Look for clear data policies, open communication, and responsive support. Avoid tools that hide how their algorithms work or collect excessive user data.

Choose partners who align with your company's ethics and values. Trust is just as important as technology.

Building Internal Buy-In and Change Management

AI adoption often fails because people resist change, not because tools fail. Involve your team early. Explain how AI helps them, not just the business.

Encourage experimentation and reward learning. When people feel included, they're more likely to explore and share success stories.

Transparency builds enthusiasm.

Testing and Iterating Before Scaling

Don't roll out AI across every department at once. Start small, track impact, and refine.

A pilot program might include automating email segmentation, improving ad optimization, or testing AI-assisted blog writing. Document what works and what doesn't. Then expand confidently.

Iteration prevents expensive mistakes and encourages continuous learning.

Avoiding Common AI Adoption Pitfalls

Three mistakes appear often:

1. Implementing tools without clear goals.
2. Ignoring team training.
3. Over-relying on automation.

AI should enhance human creativity, not suppress it. Stay flexible, stay informed, and review your systems regularly.

You're The Boss

Remember that just like running a crew, you're the boss. AI is not ready to be the CEO, foreman, or project manager. AI can do the heavy lifting and repetitive work like a champ, but it's up to you to provide the best instructions (prompts) and to oversee the results and fix any mistakes.

Sustaining Momentum via Continuous Learning

AI evolves fast. What works today might look outdated in six months. Create a learning culture that keeps everyone curious.

Set time for workshops, webinars, and internal sharing sessions. Encourage staff to explore new tools and present findings.

When curiosity becomes part of your company's DNA, adaptation becomes natural.

Takeaway Summary

- Start with an honest assessment of your current marketing process.
- Integrate AI gradually and connect all data channels properly.
- Budget for both tools and team education.
- Define success metrics before scaling.
- Keep learning so your strategy grows with technology strategically.

AI Tools to Explore

ZAPIER

- **(https://zapier.com):** connects apps and automates workflows without coding.

HUBSPOT AI

- **(https://www.hubspot.com):** manages multi-channel campaigns, predictive analytics, and CRM automation.

AIRTABLE

- **(https://airtable.com):** blends spreadsheet simplicity with automation and AI categorization.

GOOGLE LOOKER STUDIO
- **(https://lookerstudio.google.com):** turns analytics data into visual dashboards that track AI performance.

ASANA INTELLIGENCE
- **(https://asana.com):** uses AI to assign priorities, summarize updates, and predict project timelines.

Chapter 12: The Next Five Years: Where We're Headed

AI's Next Leap: From Assistants to Advisors

AI is moving from tool to teammate. Today it follows instructions. Soon it will give advice, offer strategy, and even make decisions within defined limits.

Marketing platforms already recommend budgets, content angles, and ad placement. The next step is predictive reasoning; AI suggesting campaign strategies before you ask.

This evolution will make AI feel less like software and more like a trusted colleague.

Search, Chat, and Commerce Merge

The line between searching, chatting, and buying is disappearing. When users ask a question in Google, ChatGPT, or a voice assistant, they'll soon see a seamless path to purchase.

Imagine asking, "What's the best air purifier for allergies?" and the AI instantly showing top-rated products, verified reviews, and direct checkout links; all in the same window.

For businesses, this means optimizing not just for discovery, but for decision-making. Visibility and conversion will happen in the same interaction.

Voice Search Becomes the Default Interface

Typing is giving way to talking. Within a few years, most online searches will be conversational. Smart speakers, vehicles, and even appliances will connect people to the web through speech.

Brands that master natural-language content will dominate. The winners will sound helpful, friendly, and confident; like experts who understand real human needs.

Voice-first experiences will define the next era of discoverability.

Artificial General Intelligence (AGI) and Marketing Automation

Artificial General Intelligence (AGI) is still emerging, but progress is steady. Once AI systems can understand complex context and make independent judgments, marketing will change again.

Campaigns may become self-managing. AI could test hundreds of creative directions, pick the best one, and adjust messaging in real time.

The human role will shift from doing to directing. We'll focus less on creating assets and more on setting vision, ethics, and purpose.

Regulation and Ethics in a Machine-Led World

As AI grows, so will scrutiny. Governments are drafting laws around transparency, data ownership, and synthetic media.

Companies will need clear policies on how they use AI-generated content, customer data, and automation. Ethical transparency won't just prevent penalties; it will build trust with customers who expect honesty.

Brands that handle AI responsibly will stand out as trustworthy leaders.

New Marketing Roles That Will Emerge

The future will bring roles that blend creativity with technology. Expect to see job titles like:

- **AI Marketing Strategist:** combines data analysis with storytelling.
- **Prompt Designer:** crafts effective AI instructions for creative output.
- **Automation Architect:** connects marketing systems for seamless performance.
- **Ethical AI Officer:** ensures compliance and fairness in machine decision-making.

The next generation of marketers will need to think like artists, coders, and psychologists all at once.

Preparing for the Disappearance of Traditional Search

Search engines as we know them will fade. Instead of long lists of links, users will receive dynamic answers built from verified sources.

This means businesses must focus on authority, not just optimization. AI will only recommend brands it *trusts*. To stay visible, companies will need consistent expertise, original content, and a clear online identity.

Human Brands That Win in the AI Economy

Even in a world of algorithms, people still want connection. Brands with heart, humor, and authenticity will thrive.

Businesses that show their faces, tell their stories, and give back to their communities will outshine purely digital competitors.

Technology makes communication faster. Humanity makes it meaningful.

How to Stay Ahead When Change Never Stops

The speed of innovation can feel overwhelming. The key is flexibility.

Stay curious. Learn continuously. Test new tools but never lose sight of your values. AI will evolve, but integrity, creativity, and empathy will always be timeless advantages.

The future doesn't belong to the biggest or the richest; it belongs to the most adaptable.

Final Reflection: Visibility Is the New Currency

Every brand is now judged by how visible it is in a machine-driven world. AI decides what people see, but humans decide who they trust.

Your visibility depends on clarity, authenticity, and readiness to evolve.

Adapt early. Learn fast. Stay visible.

Takeaway Summary

- AI will evolve from tool to strategic advisor.
- Search, chat, and commerce will merge into one experience.
- Voice-first interaction will dominate the next wave of marketing.
- Ethical transparency will separate trusted brands from imitators.
- The most adaptable, human-centered businesses will lead the future.

AI Tools to Explore

PERPLEXITY AI

- **(https://www.perplexity.ai):** explore conversational search and AI-driven summaries to see how answers evolve.

CHATGPT

- **(https://chat.openai.com):** test multi-step prompts and observe how generative systems handle complex questions.

GOOGLE GEMINI

- **(https://gemini.google.com):** monitor AI integrations across search, chat, and shopping.

RUNWAY ML

- **(https://runwayml.com):** experiment with AI video for storytelling and future-ready brand communication.

ETHICAL OS TOOLKIT

- **(https://ethicalos.org):** free framework for preparing your company for ethical challenges in AI innovation.

Adapt or Become Invisible

The Moment We're In

We're standing at one of the biggest turning points in marketing history. Artificial intelligence is not a passing trend or a temporary disruption; it's a complete rewrite of how communication works.

Every search, ad, post, and piece of content now passes through an intelligent system that decides what matters most to each person. That system learns, adapts, and evolves faster than any human team ever could.

This moment can feel intimidating. It can also be empowering. Because while machines may handle the mechanics, humans still control the message, the emotion, and the meaning behind it.

What Has Changed

In just a few years, AI transformed every corner of digital marketing. Search engines learned to understand context. Paid media became predictive. Content creation accelerated. Social platforms evolved into emotion-driven ecosystems.

Customers now interact with brands through voice, chat, and personalized experiences. AI filters the noise so people see what feels most relevant; and in doing so, it rewards clarity, authenticity, and trust.

Visibility is no longer just about being online. It's about being *understood* by machines and *trusted* by people.

What Hasn't Changed

The core of good marketing remains the same: honesty, empathy, and human connection. AI may help you reach audiences faster, but what keeps them engaged is still authenticity.

No matter how advanced the algorithm is, people buy from people they like and trust. They respond to stories that feel true. They stay loyal to brands that make them feel seen.

Technology can amplify your message, but it can't invent sincerity. That comes from you.

The Human Role Moving Forward

In this new era, marketers have become translators between two worlds: human language and machine logic. Your job is to teach AI what makes your brand real and valuable.

That means organizing your content so algorithms can understand it, while writing with warmth so people enjoy it. It means analyzing performance data but still listening to intuition.

Machines deliver precision. Humans deliver perspective. Both are necessary. Together, they create something stronger than either could alone.

Building for the Future

The companies that thrive will treat AI not as a replacement, but as a collaborator. They'll automate routine work so they can focus on creativity, strategy, and empathy, while always enhancing results to ensure they resonate with potential customers.

Small businesses, especially, have an advantage. They can adopt new tools quickly, pivot fast, and tell authentic stories without layers of bureaucracy. Agility will beat scale with proper implementation.

The winners of tomorrow will be the ones who learn continuously, stay curious, and act early.

How to Stay Visible

To remain visible in a machine-driven marketplace, three qualities matter most:

Clarity: Say who you are, what you offer, and why it matters; plainly and consistently.

Authenticity: Be transparent. Let your brand's real personality show.

Adaptability: Keep learning, testing, and refining your strategy.

You don't need to master every tool or trend. You just need to move forward faster than the fear that holds your competitors back.

Reframing the Relationship with AI

AI is not here to erase creativity. It's here to remove friction.

It gives marketers more time to think, experiment, and focus on what humans do best: solving problems and inspiring action.

When you see AI as a partner instead of a threat, you open the door to limitless growth.

Let it handle the heavy lifting. You handle the heart.

The New Definition of Success

In the coming years, success will look different. It won't be about who spends the most, posts the most, or ranks first on every search page. It will be about who adapts gracefully and earns lasting trust in a world that's always shifting.

You can't control every algorithm. But you can control how clearly and consistently you show up. AI rewards brands that act with purpose, clarity, and reliability.

The Invisible Risk

Businesses that ignore AI aren't just missing out; they're slowly fading from view. The internet no longer waits for slow adopters. It evolves daily.

If your brand doesn't appear in AI-driven results, conversations, or recommendations, it may as well not exist.

Invisibility is not a lack of effort. It's a lack of adaptation.

The Path Forward

Start small. Experiment with one tool or one process. Maybe automate reporting, test AI content outlines, or use predictive analytics to refine targeting.

Each small win builds confidence. Each improvement compounds.
You'll find that AI doesn't remove your role; it magnifies it. It gives you more power to lead, create, and connect.

As technology becomes smarter, authenticity becomes rarer and, therefore, more valuable.

The Last Word

Artificial intelligence has changed the landscape of marketing, but not its soul. You don't need to be a coder or a futurist to thrive in this era. You just need to stay curious, stay honest, and stay visible.

Adaptation is no longer optional. It's the new form of survival.

The future belongs to the humans who work *with* machines, not against them.

So, keep learning. Keep experimenting. And when the world changes again, as it surely will, you'll already be ready. Recognize the cycle and adapt.

Takeaway Summary

- AI isn't replacing marketers. It's amplifying them.
- Visibility requires clarity, authenticity, and adaptability.
- The human first role is to guide machines with empathy and purpose. Our second role is to check the work, always.
- Small, consistent adaptation builds long-term success.
- The brands that embrace change will define the next era of marketing.

Author's Note

When I began working in digital marketing, things were simpler. Success came from hard work, consistency, and a few well-chosen keywords. We measured rankings, watched analytics, and tried to understand what search engines wanted from us.

Then artificial intelligence arrived and changed everything...

For the first time, marketers found themselves not just optimizing for algorithms, but *collaborating* with them. We went from predicting Google to partnering with it. The pace of change has been astonishing, even for those of us who have spent our careers in this field.

What hasn't changed is the reason we do this work. Marketing has always been about connection: understanding what people care about and finding better ways to serve them. AI may change how we deliver that connection, but it can't replace why it matters.

I wrote this book because I saw too many good businesses falling behind; not for lack of talent or dedication, but for lack of clarity. The technology felt intimidating, and the advice out there often sounded either overly technical or too vague to act on. I wanted to create a guide that cuts through the noise, written in plain English, for the everyday business owner who simply wants to stay relevant.

You don't need a Ph.D. in computer science to understand AI. You just need curiosity and a willingness to evolve. The tools in this book are not magic; they're multipliers. They amplify your effort, but they still depend on your insight, creativity, and integrity.

I've seen firsthand how small adjustments; an automated ad system here, an AI-assisted blog outline there; can completely transform efficiency. But I've also seen how quickly people lose touch when they rely too heavily on automation. The sweet spot lies in balance: human-led, AI-empowered marketing.

If there's one message I hope stays with you, it's this: Adapting is not about chasing every new tool. It's about staying open, learning as you go, and keeping your humanity at the center of it all.

AI is a powerful ally, but people still respond to people. Your warmth, your honesty, and your perspective will always be your greatest marketing assets.

So keep them close.

Use technology to serve **and enhance** your creativity, not define it.

And remember that the most important intelligence in business will always be human.

Recommended Resources

AI and Digital Marketing Tools

CHATGPT
- **(https://chat.openai.com):** conversational AI for brainstorming, writing, and marketing strategy.

PERPLEXITY AI
- **(https://www.perplexity.ai):** real-time search and citation-based answer engine.

GOOGLE GEMINI
- **(https://gemini.google.com):** Google's integrated AI suite for search, productivity, and data analysis.

JASPER
- **(https://www.jasper.ai):** AI copywriting platform designed for businesses and creative teams.

HUBSPOT AI
- **(https://www.hubspot.com):** AI-driven CRM and marketing automation tools for small to mid-size businesses.

SEO and Generative Search

SEARCH ENGINE JOURNAL
- **(https://www.searchenginejournal.com):** articles, trends, and updates about modern SEO and AI search.

MOZ BLOG
- **(https://moz.com/blog):** practical strategies for improving rankings and understanding search intent.

GOOGLE SEARCH CENTRAL
- **(https://developers.google.com/search):** official documentation and updates from Google's search team.

BRIGHTLOCAL
- **(https://www.brightlocal.com):** tools for local SEO tracking, review management, and location-based marketing.

SCHEMA.ORG
- **(https://schema.org):** standards for structured data to help AI understand website content.

Advertising and PPC

GOOGLE ADS HELP CENTER
- **(https://support.google.com/google-ads):** tutorials and feature updates for Smart Bidding and Performance Max.

OPTMYZR
- **(https://www.optmyzr.com):** automation software that gives marketers control over AI-driven PPC.

META BUSINESS HELP
- **(https://www.facebook.com/business/help):** resources for running AI-optimized campaigns on Facebook and Instagram.

MICROSOFT ADVERTISING BLOG
- **(https://about.ads.microsoft.com):** insights into predictive advertising and search trends on Bing and LinkedIn.

Creative and Visual AI

MIDJOURNEY
- **(https://www.midjourney.com):** text-to-image generation for branding and concept design.

RUNWAY ML
- **(https://runwayml.com):** AI tools for video creation and content editing.

ADOBE FIREFLY
- **(https://www.adobe.com/products/firefly.html):** generative design features integrated into Adobe Creative Cloud.

CANVA MAGIC STUDIO
- **(https://www.canva.com/magic/):** accessible AI tools for quick, branded design work.

Learning and Continuing Education

MARKETING AI INSTITUTE

- **(https://www.marketingaiinstitute.com):** education and events focused on responsible AI in marketing.

THINK WITH GOOGLE

- **(https://www.thinkwithgoogle.com):** research and insights on digital behavior and advertising innovation.

COURSERA AI FOR EVERYONE

- **(https://www.coursera.org/learn/ai-for-everyone):** introductory course explaining AI's role in business.

HARVARD BUSINESS REVIEW

- **(https://hbr.org):** practical articles on AI leadership, ethics, and organizational transformation.

Let's Talk

We'd love to show you what's possible with your business. Whether you want:
- A free review of your current website or ad campaign
- A competitor audit to see who's outranking you & why
- Or just a no-pressure conversation about your goals

We're here.

Just **Scan the QR code** at the bottom of this page or visit AllegiantDigital.com to book a free digital visibility audit.

We'll give you real answers, zero fluff.

Remember This: You don't need to be the biggest company in town to win online.

You just need to be the most visible, the most trusted, and the quickest to respond. And when you do that, your schedule fills up, your stress goes down, and your business becomes what you always knew it could be. Let's make it happen.

About the Author

Chad Markham is a recognized leader in the world of digital marketing and the CEO of Allegiant Digital Marketing, a full-service agency backed by 24 years of industry success. Known for his deep expertise in SEO, SEM, social media strategy, and web development, Chad has helped thousands of businesses—from scrappy startups to Fortune 500 giants—grow their digital presence and drive real results.

From 2021 through 2024, Chad has also served as a Digital Marketing Instructor at the University of Texas at Austin, where he shared his real-world insights with the next generation of marketing professionals. His approach blends strategic thinking with a passion for innovation, making him a trusted advisor to brands and business owners alike.

Outside the office, Chad is a devoted family man, a passionate music enthusiast, and proudly holds an unofficial title as one of Austin's resident billiards sharks. He lives by the Zig Ziglar quote: "You will get all you want in life, if you help enough other people get what they want."

Made in the USA
Coppell, TX
28 February 2026

72496979R00066